THE AMERICAN
COWBOY

THE AMERICAN COWBOY

A PHOTOGRAPHIC HISTORY

EDITED BY
RICHARD COLLINS

INTRODUCTION BY
BOB EDGAR

THE LYONS PRESS

GUILFORD, CONNECTICUT

An imprint of The Globe Pequot Press

Originally published in 1996 by Salamander Books, London.

Printed in Spain

Editor: Richard Collins
Designer: Mark Holt
Film set by SX Composing DTP
Reproduction by P & W Graphics, Singapore

2 4 6 8 10 9 7 5 3

ISBN 1-58574-491-3

The Library of Congress Cataloging-in-Publication Data
is available on file.

'One looked about and said,
"This is the last West." It was not so.
There was no more West after that.
It was a dream and a forgetting,
a chapter forever closed.'

INTRODUCTION

by

**Bob Edgar, Historian, Archaeologist and Curator of the
Museum of the Old West at Old Trail Town, Cody, Wyoming**

IT IS A BEAUTIFUL FALL MORNING in the Greybull River country of northwest Wyoming. The rugged, snow-covered peaks of the Absaroka Mountains shine brightly against the clear blue sky. Ancient pine forests clothe the lower slopes and valleys. Fingers of pine and aspen, with their yellow leaves, decorate the spring-fed streams that lead to the river. The grassy foothills blend their way into the seemingly endless buffalo grass-covered prairie. Scattered through the yellow cured grass is the gray-green sage, which lends a uniquely pleasant odor to the gentle morning breeze. The twentieth century is young and the bones of the great buffalo herds, the last of which were destroyed only about forty years before by both whites and Indians, still lie on the prairie and in the hills.

A man on horseback, just a speck at first, comes riding across the vast prairie. He is a trail hardened cowboy working for the Pitchfork Ranch, which was established on the Greybull River, in what was then Wyoming Territory, by County Otto Franc Von Lichtenstein in 1878. The rider is out locating cattle in preparation for the fall roundup, when the cattle will be gathered and worked through a system of corrals. The cattle that will be sold and shipped that fall are separated out. They will then be trailed to the railroad at the relatively new eastern markets.

As the lone cowboy rides across the prairie he is suddenly startled by a roar overhead. He turns in the saddle to observe an airplane. Contemplating the arrival of a new era, he rides on, thinking about the airplane and the increasing use of the automobile and the few wooden oil derricks that have appeared on the cattle ranges. An uneasy feeling of apprehension and foreboding comes over the range rider as he goes on his way. He loves the rolling prairie, broken here and there with rocky ridges partly covered with pine, juniper and cedar; the clear streams and rivers that tumble down through the mountain canyons and into the valleys. Men of this kind love the wildness of nature. The severe blizzards of winter on the northern plains and mountains give the man of the outdoors a greater appreciation for the gentleness of a warm April morning, and for the sight of a new born calf resting on the green tender grass of spring.

Like the Indians, and all people of the outdoors, the cowboy of the plains and mountains of western America is a spiritual being. In the days of the open range, long before the introduction of barbed wire, sometimes referred to as the 'Devil's Hatband', a good many cowboys never saw the inside of a church. However, an old-time cowboy in Wyoming once said 'My church is in the mountain and my God is nature'. The cowboy, like the Indian, believes in what he sees. The Indian believes that the new year begins with the first sound of thunder in the spring. The warm sun brings up the new grass, the young are born and life is renewed. The buffalo eat the grass and man eats the buffalo. Then when a person dies and is buried in a shallow grave, the grass grows higher on the grave. The buffalo eat the grass and the cycle is complete.

In 1883, Tazwel Woody, an old cowboy of the Greybull River country, was guiding Archibald Rogers, the owner of the –TL ranch, where Woody was the foreman, on a mountain sheep hunt in the mountains of the upper Greybull River. They were at an elevation of over 12,000 feet, and were sneaking over a ridge just before dawn. Rogers was a little ahead of Woody and spotted a large ram and whispered to the old range rider to come. At that instant, the first red light of dawn hit the snow covered-peaks above them. Woody returned, 'Be quiet, God's waking!'

The cowboy of the open range days and of the early 1900s was a man of the outdoors; and, like nature, he could be very gentle and easy going. But, on the other hand, if he was wronged, he could be a dangerous enemy. If he liked you, he would do almost anything to help you; and if he did not, you had better leave him alone.

After the turn of the twentieth century, there were a number of the old cowboys still alive who had made the trail drives from Texas to Wyoming and Montana with longhorn cattle. There were others who trailed cattle back into Wyoming from Oregon. The ancestors of these cattle crossed the plains during the 1850s with the pioneer settlers on the Oregon Trail. The old weathered veterans of the plains and mountains spent their last years out on some remote ranch, doing whatever work they could, or in some western town sitting around a cafe or bar, or visiting with friends. Others may have lived out their old age with family. But their numbers dwindled as the years passed and by 1940 most of these early range riders were in their graves which are scattered throughout the western states, from Mexico to the Canadian border. Some lie buried on the plains, others in remote ranch graveyards and the rest in the old sections of town cemeteries across the west. Many are in unmarked graves. Fortunately, quite a few of these men wrote down their unique stories, and others related their experiences to someone who at least made an effort to record them. We, who came later, are deeply indebted to these people of vision who recognized the importance of recording this epic period in western America, a time which would only happen once in the history of the world.

Another small but far-sighted fraternity were the photographers who could see the importance of recording the images of the cattle drives, the frontier towns, the roundup camps, the cowboys on the range, branding cattle, the chuckwagons, the camp cooks and a variety of other circumstances. These recorders of our history deserve even more credit for their contributions not least because of the effort that it took to transport the heavy, awkward cameras, tripods, glass plates, developing solutions and other paraphernalia involved with making a photograph at that time. The cameras they used required a proper negative. The early photographers of the West only had one emulsion. It was a 'wet' one. They poured the emulsion over the glass plates in a make-shift darkroom, a tent, covered wagon, or under a canvas or blanket, or whatever, just before taking the photograph. It took quite a while to prepare the glass plate, and the more even the coating was, the less exposure time was necessary. This was a great advantage with action shots. In the 1880s, a dry emulsion, based on gelatin, was developed. This was faster. However, you did have to know what you were doing. All of this had to be transported by wagon or by pack horse, which was very risky for the equipment.

Among the early photographers who spent a substantial part of their lives trying to record for posterity this dramatic period of history were Huffman, Kendrick, Smith, Koerner and Belden. The cattleman's frontier, from the end of the Civil War to the early 1900s, will never come again. It seems that the best way to get a feel for those times and the men who lived them is to present, in part, some of their own stories and observations.

The first attempt to drive cattle from Texas to Montana occurred in 1866. Nelson A. Story had struck it rich in the Montana gold fields in the early 1860s. He decided that he could make a profit on cattle around the gold mining communities. He cashed in his gold dust for

$40,000 and headed at the age of twenty-eight for Texas. Story bought 1,000 head of Texas longhorns and hired twenty-five of the toughest cowboys he could find to help drive the herd to Montana. They, no doubt, had plenty of hardships coming north. When they got to Fort Leavenworth, Kansas, Story purchased a train of ox-drawn wagons, which he loaded with groceries and other supplies, to establish a store in the town of Bozeman, Montana.

At Fort Laramie, he was joined by Major John B. Catlin, who provided his men with new Remington breech-loading rifles. Story and his cowboys were also carrying two Colt revolvers. The trail herd moved north. A ways from Fort Reno, the drivers came upon a Frenchman and a boy who were unharnessing their team and were in the process of making camp. Warned against hostile Indians everywhere in the area, the two were invited to join the Story party for protection. However, the Frenchman, after glancing around at Story's hard looking and well-armed cowboys, said that he had a greater fear of some white men than he had of the Indians.

As Story moved on down the Bozeman Trail, the party was attacked by Sioux Indians not far from Fort Reno. It was a hit and run attack, which left two drovers badly wounded by arrows, the Indians getting away with several cattle. The herd was stampeded, but the herders opened fire on the Sioux with their rifles and drove them off. After the cattle had been quietened down, several of the cowboys followed the Sioux and found their camp at dusk. The drovers rode in first and cut out the stolen cattle and took them back from the Indians. When the herd was reassembled, Story pushed on to Fort Reno with his wounded companions, but not until some of his herders had gone back to see about the Frenchman and the boy. They were found dead, scalped, and their bodies mutilated. Their horses were gone and their wagon burned. The herders buried the unfortunate travelers who had met such a violent death.

After a short rest at Fort Reno, the trail herd moved on, leaving the two wounded cowboys. It was getting late in the season and Story wanted to keep moving. Three miles south of Fort Phil Kearny, Story was stopped by Colonel Carrington, who would not allow the herd to come any closer. He claimed that the grass close to the post was needed for his own livestock, and ordered Story to corral the cattle until a wagon train could come along with at least forty armed men.

After being held up for two weeks, Story and his men left one night, against military orders. During the remainder of the drive, the herd grazed during the day and pushed forward at night. As they traveled up the trail, they were attacked two more times by Sioux Indians.

Both times they held them off with their breech-loading rifles and Colt revolvers. Only one man was lost. He carelessly rode too far ahead and was killed and scalped. He was buried on the prairie. On 9 December 1866, Story's spectacular cattle drive reached its destination near the present site of Livingston, Montana, where he established a permanent cattle camp.

The next account was written by cowboy Frank Canton, describing part of a cattle drive from Denton County, Texas, to Abilene, Kansas, in 1869.

'Jerry Burnett was an old settler and cattleman and Captain M.B. Lloyd, got together a herd of fifteen hundred head of cattle to drive to Abilene, Kansas. Burk Burnett was then a young lively cowboy and he was placed in charge of the herd. He asked me to go with him, saying that I would need four good cow ponies. I agreed to go. I got my ponies and equipment on the trail with a herd of cattle. I soon found that I had a great deal to learn, but was willing to work, and by close attention, managed to do my part.

We drove our cattle to the Rock Crossing on Red River. We found the river was bank full, and this meant that we would have to swim every inch of the way across. To anyone who has ever seen the South Canadian, or the Red River, on a rampage, this description will seem weak and meager compared to their impressions. These streams have their sources in the great canyons of the Rocky Mountains. The spring rains and thaws helped fill these canyons with water that goes rolling down out of the mountains onto the river beds of the plains, and the great supply does not exhaust itself until these streams empty into the larger rivers below. These flood waters become mixed with the great bed of quicksand, which makes it difficult for either a man or beast to swim in. It is more than forty years ago, yet I distinctly remember how the old Red River was cutting up on this occasion. The waters were rushing swiftly, carrying uprooted trees and other debris down the current. In places great waves dashing against a sandbar of some shallow place would throw spouting sheets of water into the air. It was a seething maelstrom. I did not wonder that the cattle refused to be driven into this water. For I confess that it did not look safe to try to swim it. Cattle are very hard to drown and will swim longer than a horse; but sometimes after they get into the water, the leaders will turn back and the whole bunch begin to swim in a circle, and the herd will follow the leaders just as they do in a stampede, and this circle must be broken or they will all drown.

Finally we cut off a good bunch of the leaders and drove them into the water. They headed towards the opposite shore, with Tib Burnett, brother of Burk, swimming ahead of them on his pony. The rest of us were all working to drive the herd into the river before the leaders landed on the opposite side, but they got scared and it was impossible to make them take the water. We worked four days before we succeeded in getting the entire herd across. We tried to start them at nearly every curve in the river until we reached what was known as Spanish Fork Bend, above Gainsville. Here we started the whole herd towards the river and made the cattle in the rear crowd the leaders off into the water. One of our cowboys was ready and leaped in with his horse and started to swim ahead of the cattle to pilot them across. They began to follow him and more of the cattle began to jump in, for now that the leaders had started, they all wanted to go. In twenty minutes the whole herd was swimming in a straight line for the opposite bank, but the current was so swift that we landed about a mile down the river. Our loose horses swam over, and we made a raft heavy enough to hold up our mess wagon, which we drifted over safely.

After we crossed the river we went into camp to dry out. Tib Burnett, who had crossed over several days before at the Rock Crossing, had thrown in his bunch of cattle with another cow outfit and started on the trail ahead of us. We did not see him again until we reached Abilene, Kansas.

The rainy season had set in and we had a hard trip for the first ten days in the Indian Territory. Electric storms and heavy rain caused the cattle to commence stampeding, which kept us in the saddle day and night. When we had a chance for a little sleep, we would drop down on our wet saddle blankets and cover with our slickers. I did not have a dry stitch of clothes on for a week. We passed near the west slope of the Arbuckle Mountains, and angled across the country in a northwesterly direction until we struck the Chisholm Trail. Since the country we traveled over, which is now western Oklahoma, is settled up so thickly, I cannot locate just where the trail ran. We did not know the names of the streams we crossed, and had to swim most of them. Not a soul lived in the country on our route; nothing but buffalo, antelope, deer, wild turkey, lobo wolves and coyotes. The rainy weather seemed to be over. The sun came out. Our cattle were now well broken to the trail and we had a chance to catch up on sleep. We congratulated ourselves on not having seen an Indian on the trip. Other outfits ahead of us had not been so lucky. Many other herds had been stampeded by Indians and several cowboys had been killed. We were getting up north in the Indian Territory, I think it was about twenty miles from the Kansas line. We had stopped the mess wagon for dinner. A short distance away was a tall bluff overlooking a small creek. I rode down by the bluff and dismounted to gather some wild sand plums. I looked up and saw two Indians on a bluff above me, about fifty yards away, their faces painted. They sat on their horses watching me, but neither of us said a word. Finally, I jumped on my cow pony and spurred him for camp.

After I reported to Burk Burnett what I had seen, we hurried to the wagon and examined what few guns we had and found that they were very rusty from the wet weather and in no condition for service. We had brought along with us some old Henry rifles, which were rimfire and not much good, but we all had good Colt six-shooters with plenty of ammunition. We had scarcely got our rifles cleaned and loaded when about twenty-five mounted Indians came galloping down toward the herd. We mounted our horses and began to ride around the cattle so as to bunch them closely. The Indians rode up to us. They and their horses were covered with war paint. They were Osages. Each Indian had a bow and quiver of arrows with steel heads, and they were also armed with good rifles and ammunition. One Indian, who could talk broken English, said that his tribe owned all that country and they demanded one hundred head of cattle for allowing us to drive our herd over their buffalo range. We then held a conference and decided that we could stand off this bunch of twenty-five if it came to a showdown.

About this time, war bonnets began to show up all along the horizon. I think about two hundred Indians altogether rode down towards us from the top of the ridge about a quarter of a mile away. When the chief learned that we would not give up the cattle, he made a sign to the Indians and they rode into the herd and killed six cattle with the bow and arrow, the same as they kill buffalo. We made no effort to stop them, but commenced to drift our herd to the north. I have often wondered why they allowed us to escape with our scalps.

After the Indians left us, we drove our herd about eight miles farther north and went into camp for the night on the south bank of the Kaw River. After having the cattle bedded down for the night, we arranged for the detail of night herders. The horse wrangler was directed to take the loose horses away, not far from the cattle, and herd them for the night. We were not exactly expecting trouble, for we supposed the Indians were satisfied, yet we decided to keep on the watch. Each man picketed one cow pony near the wagon and the rest were all turned loose in the horse herd. We spread our blankets down on the buffalo grass and turned in. It was a moonlit night, with not a sound to be heard except the occasional howl of the lobo wolf, or the quick, short yelp of the coyote. The two night herders kept up a chanting song as they rode back and forth around the herd. This singing seems to have a soothing and quieting effect upon the cattle as they are resting for the night. The cattle had plenty of time to graze before we bedded them, and were now all lying down at rest; probably not more than a half dozen in the big herd were standing up.

In the middle of the night, I was awakened by a deep rumbling noise of a stampede. This is a sound that the cowboy never mistakes for anything else and always dreads to hear. I sprang to my feet instantly and ran for my horse, saddle and bridle in hand. Burk Burnett had gotten on his feet first, snatched up his bridle and jumped on his horse bareback. He was riding like the wind to head off the leaders of the herd. I followed Burk at top speed. The cattle strung out along beside us, their glistening horns clattering together making a sound like hail falling on a tin roof as they crowded, snorted and raced headlong over the prairie. We knew that we could not stop them, but if we could turn the leaders, we would have them running in a circle until they would wind themselves up like the coils of a snail shell. I drew up even with Burk, and he caught up with the leaders and was whipping them over the side of the head with his quirt. Finally, we succeeded in turning the leaders until they were following as much as they were leading. They turned and kept on turning and those that followed them also turned, until they were at last brought to a stop. They packed themselves up so tightly that those in the center of the bunch could hardly move. Then we quieted them down by singing to them as we circled the herd. Some of them had their horns broken off, and a few had broken legs, but we had them anyway.

Sometime after the stampede, the two night herders came in one at a time from across the prairie and reported that our cattle had been stampeded by the Indians. The next morning the horse wrangler, who was very badly scared, showed up with the news that the Indians had run off our entire herd of saddle horses. The Indians had virtually set us afoot, as we had only the horses that we had picked out the night before, and these we had to save for night work. There was nothing for us to do but drive on foot in the daytime as we could not buy horses anyplace along the trail. Then commenced the hardest trip of my life...❞

(Excerpt from *Frontier Trails: The Autobiography of Frank M.Canton,*
edited by Edward Everett Dale, University of Oklahoma Press, Norman, 1966)

Another trail herd was moving up the Texas Trail, a few years later, when they almost lost their horse herd to the Indians. Three of the cowboys discovered the Indians and the horse herd moving. Unfortunately their rifles were in the chuckwagon, too far away to get to in time. They were wearing their six-shooters, so they ran as hard as they could and climbed onto a grassy hill where they could see the country around them. They immediately laid in the grass and began firing with their new forty-five Colt revolvers at the Indians who were driving the horse herd ahead of them. Some of the Indians swung around and returned the fire with their rifles. Their bullets knocked dirt and dust into the air from the edge of the hill in front of the desperate men, lying in the grass. The cowboys kept loading and firing their six-shooters and were having a demoralizing effect on the Indians, even from long range. Two of the Indian horses were killed and one of the warriors was also hit. The sound of the guns brought the men running from camp. When they spotted their horses moving, and saw the Indians, they opened fire with their rifles. The Indians soon abandoned the horses and retreated into the nearby hills. When the cowboys on the hill stood up to motion to their companions, they noticed that the grass in front of them was burned off by gunfire from their forty-five Colts. Later, they breathed a big sigh of relief when they found out that the Indians did not get their horse herd. For the cowboys of the open range days, the six-shooter was one of their most important possessions, especially after the development of the 1873 Colt into the forty-five long Colt cartridge. In the hands of an experienced shot, the forty-five Colt is effective at 100 yards and even much farther. The six-shooter is much easier to carry and use on horseback than a rifle. Also, it can be carried in an open holster on a belt that holds forty to fifty cartridges. In wet weather, the gun stays dry under the rider's coat or slicker, always within reach. Most men could carry a six-shooter all their life and never have to use it to defend themselves; but for the feeling of security in a wild country at a dangerous and lawless time, it was worth the price. Also, cowboys could help turn a stampeding herd by firing their six-shooters, or quickly stop the suffering of injured animals. The six-shooter was sometimes used for sending signals from a distance, where a pre-determined number of shots had a meaning.

It is impossible to comprehend the human experience that transpired along these cattle trails. It has been estimated that 25,000 to 35,000 men trailed six to ten million head of cattle and a million horses northward from Texas to Kansas and on through the territories as far as the Canadian line. This incredible epic began at the end of the Civil War and lasted until about the turn of the twentieth century.

Most of the Texas cattle that entered Wyoming did so at Pine Bluffs, on the Texas Trail in the late 1870s. The first Texas cattle to arrive in Montana, with the exception of Nelson Story's, were in the fall of 1881. This was an English outfit that trailed to the mouth of Otter

Creek on the Tongue River. Prior to this, most of the cattle in western Montana were from Oregon and eastern Washington. Through the 1880s and 1890s, cattle ranches were located on the Yellowstone, Clarks Fork, Mussleshell, Missouri, Tongue, and Little Missouri rivers, along with many of their tributaries.

About this same time, cattle ranches were being established in eastern Wyoming and west to the Big Horn Mountains. Most of the big speculators and investors in the cattle business in the western states were English, Scottish, French, a few Germans and, of course, Americans, a good many from Texas. At first a substantial number of cowboys were from Texas, New Mexico, Utah and eventually from all over. The first ranches of both Montana and Wyoming ran their cattle and horses on the open range. There were millions of acres of unfenced natural country. The cattle were branded with their owners' brand, but they roamed unrestricted over the entire landscape and the various owners' cattle became mixed. Two big roundups took place each year and cowboys from each ranch, who had cattle within a given region, worked together to gather several thousand head of cattle.

The representatives from the different ranches met at a rendezvous point for the spring roundup. There could be up to 100 cowboys, several chuckwagons and cooks, several hundred head of saddle horses, and a half dozen or more supply wagons that hauled the cowboys, beds, extra groceries, provisions, branding irons and sometimes even grain for the horses. This army of men and horses systematically moved across the land. The cowboys spread out over hills and prairie and gathered all the cattle, bringing them to a designated spot. The cattle were then separated by the brand of the owner's ranch. The calves that were with the mother cows were then roped and pulled to the branding fire, where the branding irons were kept hot. The calf was branded and released with the brand of its mother and of the home ranch. This process went on for weeks as the roundup crew kept moving on. The same process was more or less repeated in the early fall. The cattle were gathered and separated again; however, the 'reps', as the cowboys were called, separated out the cattle that the home ranch would trail to some point on the railroad where they would be loaded on cattle cars and shipped to market, usually Chicago.

The Big Horn Basin of northwest Wyoming was the last major region of the northern plains and mountains to be opened from Indian country. The region was barely open in 1878, when the first speculators and investors were searching for ranch sites. Count Otto Franc Von Lichtenstein was one of five men who decided on a ranch location that year. Backed by family money, Franc contracted for 1,000 head of Hereford cattle in the Gallatin Valley of western Montana that winter. Franc contracted with Jack Wiggins to hire his own cowboys and trail the herd to the Greybull River and the new site of the Pitchfork Ranch. For obvious reasons, Wiggins chose not to cross the Crow Indian land along the Yellowstone River to the north. He moved that trail herd down through Idaho, back over South Pass in the Wind River Mountains, across the Wind River and over the Owl Creek Mountains into the Big Horn Basin and the Greybull River, arriving at the Pitchfork Ranch site late in the fall of 1879.

Otto Franc worked hard over the next twenty-five years and the Pitchfork Ranch became one of the success stories of the region. Franc learned to establish irrigated fields to raise hay for winter cattle feed after the brutal winter of 1886–87, which killed cattle by the thousands across the northern plains. Franc and the cowboys who he employed worked hard and by the mid-1890s the Pitchfork Ranch was shipping several thousand head of fat cattle at Billings, Montana, on the Yellowstone River.

Otto Franc was found dead from a gun shot wound not far from his home on 29 November 1903. An existing range war between sheep and cattlemen was believed to be the cause. He was buried in Meeteetse, Wyoming.

After Franc's death, L.G. Phelps bought the ranch from Franc's sister in Germany. After Phelps died in 1922, the Pitchfork was managed by Phelps' son Eugene, and Charles Belden, who had married Frances Phelps. It has been said that Eugene and Charles argued a lot and that Charles Belden wasted too much time on his obsession with photographing cowboys, cattle and ranch life. Thank goodness he did not quit. Over the next twenty-five years, the work that Charles Belden undertook was to leave the world a rich legacy. Belden, not unlike the photographers of earlier years, felt the urgency to record in photographs the unspoiled landscape, the cattle drives, working livestock, the old-time cowboys in action. He, like others, recorded the last glimpses of a vanishing era and the vanishing men who lived it.

Meeteetse, Wyoming, is still a cowtown. One of the few left. One day, not so many years ago, we were in Meeteetse. A man on the boardwalk caught our eye. It was obvious from his beat up, high crown Stetson, and rough weathered face, that he was an old-time cowboy. He had been a big man, but he was stooped now from time and work. We felt the desire to make his acquaintance and found that he had just been laid off at the Arapaho Ranch on Owl Creek, forty miles to the south, and his name was Hank. We know that he had a story and wanted to hear some of it. Old Hank was not much on talking but we learned that he had ridden at the Pitchfork, like many others, when Charles Belden was there. He told us that he had left Wyoming years ago and had worked on ranches from Texas to Nevada and back. Hank looked like he was telling the truth. The old man felt that we were sincere and asked if we could give him a ride. We all got into an old pickup truck and Hank directed us to a pioneer cemetery up in the hills along Meeteetse Creek. We got out and walked over to the old graves on the grass and sage brush prairie. Old Hank's bent form made its way over to a picket fence; the wooden boards were burnt brown from the sun and leaning from the winter winds. The interior of the fragile enclosure was overgrown with sage brush and a wild rose bush whose leaves had turned red from the early frost. Old Hank looked bent and weak against the distant hills, as he gently touched the weathered wood. We tried not to stare but we could not miss the tear on Old Hank's weathered cheek.

Soon he said 'We can go now'. We did not talk much, maybe not at all, on the way back to town. Hank wanted to be dropped off at a friend's place in the alley behind the restaurant. We never saw Old Hank again.

Cowboy from Matador Ranch, Texas.

Erwin E. Smith (1886–1947)

⚰ A roundup of 5,000 Matador cattle, Texas.

ERWIN E. SMITH

➤ Spur of the Matador trail herd, Texas, 1908.

ERWIN E. SMITH

Matador cowboy drinking.

ERWIN E. SMITH

Campfire, Matador Ranch.

Erwin E. Smith

♟ 'Rounding Em Up', Wyoming.

CHARLES D. KIRKLAND (1857–1926)

Chasing a yearling, Wyoming.

CHARLES D. KIRKLAND

↑ Roundup.

Charles J. Belden (1887–1966)

← Pulling a cow out of a bad place, LS Ranch, Texas.

Erwin E. Smith

→ Jack Rhodes, Senior, following a cow in snow, carrying a calf across his lap, 1938 or 1939.

Charles J. Belden

⤙ Two cowboys, 1895.

L. A HUFFMAN (1854–1931)

ES, MONT.

━ Cowboy, August 1904.

L. A. Huffman

❢ Lee Warren the Buster and his 'Hazer', September 1904.

L. A. Huffman

↑ 2 D chuckwagon, Montana prairies.

'Bacon in the pan
Coffee in the pot
Get up an' get it
Get it while it's hot!'

⚐ An old time chuckwagon in about 1885.

L. A. Huffman

↑ Roderick Munroe, the cook of the LU Bar Ranch, Montana, making bread, about 1904. Munroe came to Montana from Dingwall, Scotland, in 1889.

L. A. Huffman

← Mex John making pies.

L. A. Huffman

→ Taking a shave. A outfit, Texas.

Erwin E. Smith

⬆ End of another day.

➤ Cowboys singing at the chuckwagon.

and overleaf. Cowboys and herd near Miles City, Montana, 1894.

F. JAY HAYNES (1853–1921)

🛉 Same sequence, Montana, 1894.

F. JAY HAYNES

Same sequence, Montana, 1894.

F. Jay Haynes

Roundup – holding a herd on Big Pumpkin Creek.

L. A. Huffman

↟ and ➤ Bringing a calf to the branding fire, sequence, 1907.

L. A. HUFFMAN

◄ Branding calves in corrall, Little Pumpkin Creek, about 1890.

L. A. HUFFMAN

❧ Branding fire, Little Pumpkin Creek, 1907.

L. A. HUFFMAN

Branding. Judith River Roundup, Montana, about 1910.

Dragging a calf to branding.

UNIDENTIFIED PHOTOGRAPHER

❦ Three cowboys branding.

Branding a maverick yearling, Texas.

Erwin E. Smith

➤ Biering–Cunningham Hereford cattle on Cash Creek Basin,
divide of the Gallatin and Madison rivers, Montana, 1910.

SCHLECHTEN BROTHERS, BOZEMAN, MONTANA

Biering–Cunningham cattle on Lower Elk Creek near the Madison River, Montana, 1916.

SCHLECHTEN BROTHERS, BOZEMAN, MONTANA

◂ Indian adjusting bridle, Lodge Grass, Montana, 1927. Crow encampment for the All-Indian Rodeo, 4 July.

W. H. D. KOERNER (1878–1938)

⚐ Indian cowboy on horseback, Lodge Grass, Montana, 1927.

W. H. D KOERNER

⚓ Evening at the Roundup Camp, Big Pumpkin Creek, Montana, 1907.

L. A. Huffman

Horses crossing river. Noon beside the Roundup Camp, Hat X
outfit, July 1904.

L. A. HUFFMAN

Hat X cow camp, Hungry Creek, August 1904.

⚘ Saddling a bronco, September 1904.

L. A. HUFFMAN

⚘ Giving a bronco a slicker lesson, September 1904.

L. A. HUFFMAN

↑ Slicker lesson, continued.

L. A. Huffman

↓ Mounting a bronco, with the ear twist.

L. A. Huffman

Roping a mustang, September 1904.

L. A. HUFFMAN

Bronco busters of the LS outfit.

Erwin E. Smith

Edwin Sanders (cousin of the photographer), saddling a bronco, Three Circle Ranch, Texas.

Erwin E. Smith

Turkey Track cowboys fording the Wichita River.

Erwin E. Smith

↟ Cowboys from the Three Block Ranch, New Mexico.

ERWIN E. SMITH

XIT ('Ten-in-Texas') cowboys, members of a Texas Panhandle trail herd, 1890. Back row left to right: Steve Beebe, Frank Freeland, Billy Wilson. Front row: John Flowers, Al (Alden) Denby, Tom McHenry, Dick Mabrey, Tony (last name unknown).

WILEY BROTHERS, MILES CITY, MONTANA

◂ Elmer on horse in lake.

CHARLES J. BELDEN

↟ Stray men packing a tarp, OR outfit, Arizona.

ERWIN E. SMITH

At the limits of the range, LS Ranch line camp, Texas. Jack Burnett, in doorway, later became range boss of the outfit.

ERWIN E. SMITH

 Interior of line camp, between Pumpkin Creek and Mizpah,
Montana, 1910.

L. A. Huffman

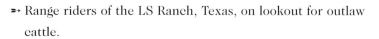 Range riders of the LS Ranch, Texas, on lookout for outlaw cattle.

ERWIN E. SMITH

<≡ Cowboy playing fiddle.

ERWIN E. SMITH

ĭ Bill Borron playing the fiddle.

CHARLES J. BELDEN

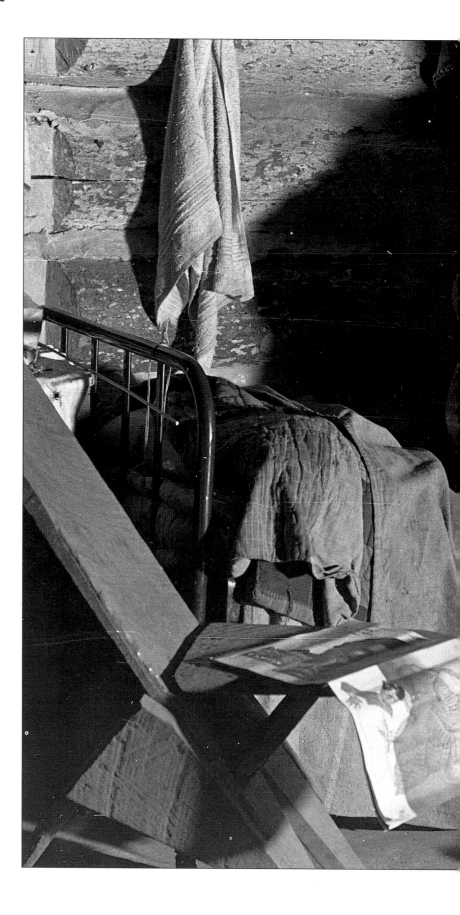

➤ Cowboy playing guitar inside cabin.

CHARLES J. BELDEN

❦ Evening relaxation.

CHARLES J. BELDEN

Pete Jakobi with fiddle, Charlie Jackson with mandolin.
Jackson's Ranch on Little Porcupine, 1902.

UNIDENTIFIED PHOTOGRAPHER

Cowboys on the prairie, Shonkin Roundup crew, 1884, near
Highwood Mountains, Fort Benton, Montana.

Dan Dutro (1848–1918)

⚘ Thomas H. Martin, early day cowpuncher and bullwacker,
1880s.

DAN DUTRO

♯ Cowboy Dunn, Hat X horse wrangler, August 1904.

L. A. HUFFMAN

↤ Roundup – probably Judith Basin, Montana. Charles M. Russell, the artist, is mounted, center, on right of rider on gray horse. Early 1880s.

UNIDENTIFIED PHOTOGRAPHER

↤ Judith Roundup, early 1880s. C.M. Russell is third man on left, front row. Utica, Montana, in background.

UNIDENTIFIED PHOTOGRAPHER

⚑ Herding cattle.

CHARLES J. BELDEN

ᛘ Throwing the herd to the bed ground – Tongue River Roundup,
1907.

L.A. Huffman

❦ Cattle on hillside.

Cowboy and cattle drinking.

CHARLES J. BELDEN

 A cowboy's funeral.

UNIDENTIFIED PHOTOGRAPHER

Cattle crossing river.

CHARLES J. BELDEN

✵ Cattle drinking, North Platte River, at Orrin, 1884.

CHARLES J. BELDEN

◄ Calves and yearlings headed for the corn belt.

CHARLES J. BELDEN

♦ Cowboy in blizzard, winter 1926–27.

CHARLES J. BELDEN

⚑ Winter cattle drive, 1920s.

CHARLES J. BELDEN

 A long, long trail a-winding.

CHARLES J. BELDEN

↑ Cattle in winter snowstorm.

CHARLES J. BELDEN

← Cowboys trailing calves to Whit Ranch, about 1933.

CHARLES J. BELDEN

Two lineriders, at JK Ranch on the Yellowstone River, February 1891.

Cowboys, at the Judith River Roundup about 1910.

↤ Buck Taylor, cowboy, about 1890.

UNIDENTIFIED PHOTOGRAPHER

↤ Gordon Sage, cowboy, about 1898.

UNIDENTIFIED PHOTOGRAPHER

Bob Chadwick, bronco buster, Rosebud, Montana, 1906.
UNIDENTIFIED PHOTOGRAPHER

Ernest Fuchs, cowboy, Mingusville, Montana, June 1899.
F. JAY HAYNES

Cowboys at lunch.

ATTRIBUTED TO C. A. KENDRICK

➤ Cowboy, third from left, riding a steer, Miles City, Montana, 1894.

F. JAY HAYNES

➤ Isadore Nollet house, 'The home of the cowboy', Mingusville, Montana, June 1890.

F. Jay Haynes

ⷜ George McClellan and dogs at home ranch, Red Bank Cattle Co.

Unidentified Photographer

➤ Ranch on the Tongue River, Montana.

L. A. Huffman

Ranch in the Missouri breaks, August 1904.

L. A. HUFFMAN

❦ Interior of ranch on the Powder River, Montana.
L.A. HUFFMAN

The Circle Bar Ranch on Otter Creek. The 'fort' on the hilltop
was built in anticipation of a Cheyenne outbreak.

L. A. HUFFMAN

◄ Hat X Cow Camp, Timber Creek, October 1902.

L. A. HUFFMAN

◄ The OW Ranch on Hanging Woman Creek, Montana, August 1880.

L. A. HUFFMAN

↑ Coming up the trail, with the beef herd, 300 miles to the shipping. Circle Roundup outfit, Valley County, Montana, 1906.

CHARLES E. MORRIS, CHINOOK, MONTANA

The photographer G. V. Barker described this photograph: 'This is the finest picture I have taken in 40 years at the business. The title of this picture is "The Last Round on the Ranges". It was the last trip of the XIT Cattle Company, gathering and shipping all their cattle and going out of business. This was taken in 1908 at the forks of Burns Creek, west of the badlands and lower Yellowstone Valley, 20 miles north of Glendive, Mont. A cavy of 165 thoroughbred saddle ponies, the finest bunch on the range. The finest cloud effects I ever got. 16 men and all in sight. Was forced to take this against the sun with white dust screen in back and shows more horses than usual. This was the first time I was ever on the range, and saw the cowboys in action. I processed 12 of the finest pictures in my collection at this time. Rufus Morse was man in charge in lead (?) cook wagon.'

G. V. BARKER, LEWISTOWN, IDAHO

ACKNOWLEDGMENTS

Salamander Books gratefully acknowledge the following institutions for allowing photographs from their collections to be reproduced in this book:

Buffalo Bill Historical Center, Cody, Wyoming: 56–57, 107 (last three gift of the artist's heirs, W. H. D. Koerner, III and Ruth Koerner Oliver), 110, 111; BBHC, Charles Belden Collection: front cover, 27, 37, 74, 81, 82, 100–106.

Colorado Historical Society, Denver, Colorado: 114–15.

Erwin E.Smith Collection, Nita Stewart Haley Memorial Library, Midland, Texas: 5, 18–23, 26 (bottom), 35, 36, 51, 54–5, 66–71, 75, 76, 78–80.

Haynes Foundation Collection, Montana Historical Society, Helena, Montana: 38–41, 113, 116–17.

Montana Historical Society, Helena, Montana: 28–34, 42–6, 59–65, 72–3, 77, 85–91, 93, 96–7, 108, 109, 112, 120–127, back cover.

Wyoming Division of Cultural Resources, Cheyenne, Wyoming: half-title, 24, 25, 26 (top), 48–50, 84, 92, 94, 95, 98, 99, 118.

In addition, the editor would like to thank Rebecca Kohl (Helena), Elizabeth Holmes (Cody), Rebecca Lintz (Denver), Hollie McHenry (Cheyenne) and Jim Bradshaw (Midland) for their kind assistance, and especially Raelen Williard of Information Now, Helena, Montana, for her picture research.

The photographs in this book were selected by the editor; responsibility for errors of choice or interpretation rests solely with him. The book intends to show, through the work of a handful of photographers, the ebb and flow of a way of life in the American West. Thanks to Mr Bob Edgar, whose Introduction captures so movingly the spirit of the whole grand adventure.

The quote on pp. 10–13 courtesy of the University of Oklahoma Press, Norman, Oklahoma, a division of the University, from the new edition copyright 1966.